# Tom and Bella Sto

## Pink Series

Author        Marlene Greenwood

Illustrator    James Greenwood

©  Marlene Greenwood    Author
©  James Greenwood    Illustrator

The moral rights of the author and illustrator have been asserted.

This book was originally published as four separate eight-paged books in 2012.

| Titles: | | |
|---|---|---|
| *Tom* | 978 1 84305 223 4 | |
| *A Big Dog* | 978 1 84305 224 1 | |
| *Bella* | 978 1 84305 225 8 | |
| *A Bad Cat* | 978 1 84305 226 5 | |

Jelly and Bean Ltd    www.jellyandbean.co.uk

ISBN 978 1 84305 414 6

# Tom and Bella Stories Pink Series

## Stories

# Information for Teachers

This book contains four separate stories for children starting to learn to read.

The vocabulary consists of simple words that are well known to children.

The eighteen most frequently occurring letters of the alphabet are introduced gradually.

The letters are a, b, c, d, e, f, g, h, i, l, m, n, o, p, r, s, t, u.

The text is made up of single words and phrases, so that punctuation is unnecessary.

The words are joined by the connecting words a, on, in, and, the

Capital letters are used in the names Tom and Bella.

The letter 's' represents two different sounds in 'cats, cups' and 'dogs, pans'.

The only 'tricky' word used is the in the last story.

| Story title | Introduction of new letters | Introduction of new words |
|---|---|---|
| *Tom* | t, o, m, c, a, t, n, d, g, s | Tom a cat on dog and (cats dogs) |
| *A Big Dog* | b, i, f | mat big tin fat |
| *Bella* | e, l, r | Bella doll rabbit bag bed |
| *A Bad Cat* | u, p, h | cup (cups) the bad pans in |

# Story 1

# Tom

Tom

a cat on Tom

# a dog on Tom

a cat and a dog

a cat on a dog

cats

dogs

Tom and cats
and dogs

Match the words to the pictures.

Tom

cat

dog

Words to learn

a  on  and

# Story 2

# A Big Dog

cats on a mat

a big dog

# a mat on cats

# Tom and a big dog

# Tom and cats
# on a mat

a big tin

# cats and a big tin

fat cats on a mat

Match the words to the pictures.

cats on a mat

a big tin

a big dog

Words to learn

a  on  big  and

# Story 3

## Bella

# Bella

# Bella and a doll

# Bella and a rabbit

# Bella and a bag

a bag on a bed

a doll on a bed

a rabbit on a bed

# Bella and a doll
# and a rabbit

Match the words to the pictures.

rabbit    Bella

doll

Words to learn

# a on in and

# Story 4

# A Bad Cat

# Bella and a cup

a cat and a cup

a bad cat

# Bella and the
# bad cat

the bad cat
on the pans

the bad cat
on the cups

pans and cups

the bad cat
in the bin

Can you see a cup?     Can you see a cat?

Can you see a pan?     Can you see Bella?

Words to learn

a   on   in   and   the

Printed in Great Britain
by Amazon

15289478R00027